WHISPERS *of the* MANGROVES

For Radhika's Dada and Chetna's MG,
who inspired us to dream.

First published in India by HarperCollins Children's Books 2025
An imprint of HarperCollins Publishers
HarperCollins Publishers India, Cyber City,
Building 10-A, Gurugram, Haryana-122002, India
www.harpercollins.co.in

2 4 6 8 10 9 7 5 3 1

Written by Radhika Suri and Chetna Singh Kaith
Illustrated by Pari Satarkar
Designed by Somesh Kumar
Specialist: Laxmikant Deshpande

P-ISBN: 978-93-6989-409-3
E-ISBN: 978-93-6213-306-9

Typeset in 17/22 Parry
by HarperCollins Publishers India Pvt. Ltd

Printed and bound at
Nutech Print Services - India

HarperCollins Publishers, Macken House, 39/40 Mayor Street Upper,
Dublin 1, D01 C9W8, Ireland

WHISPERS *of the* MANGROVES

Radhika Suri and
Chetna Singh Kaith

Illustrated by
Pari Satarkar

Magical Mangrove Hugs! ♡ Radhika & Chetna

HARPERCOLLINS
CHILDREN'S BOOKS

A forest hugs our Earth tight,
where warm sand meets salty waves.

This is the mangrove—
a place of wonder and mystery,
where every whisper tells a story.

WHISPERS OF THE BREATHING ROOTS

Mangroves grow where most plants can't.

Their leaves remove salt,
and their roots breathe air.
Some roots poke out
like pencils in the mud.
Others twist and turn like a maze.

Stilt-like roots lift them high along
the shoreline.

WHISPERS BENEATH THE WATER

Roots, spread out like umbrellas,
are a playground for baby fish,
crabs, and shrimp!

Thousands of shimmering fish
dart and swirl while
the jellyfish
rests upside down.

Starfish, oysters, and snails
cling to the roots.

And an archerfish aims
with its sharp eyes.
Whoosh! It squirts water
to knock bugs off the tree.

WHISPERS OF THE SEAGRASS

In the shallow blue waters, gentle dugongs glide.
These sea cows nibble on the soft green grass all day.

Green turtles drift,
and seahorses cling to swaying grass.

The seagrass protects the mangroves from big waves, and mangroves help keep them clean.

WHISPERS IN THE MUDFLATS

In the brown, muddy swamp,
creatures dig and burrow, bringing the mud to life.

A fiddler crab scuttles by, waving its big claw.

The mudskipper hops, rolls, wiggles,
and even climbs a tree—
at home in water and on land.

WHISPERS OF THE WINGS

Flamingos stand tall,
their bright pink feathers
brightening up the shallow waters.

A striated heron
drops a feather as bait,
frozen and sharp-eyed,
waiting for a catch.

Then, a flash of blue!
A kingfisher swoops down to grab a tiny fish!

WHISPERS FROM AN ISLAND

On a tiny island lives a rare
pygmy three-toed sloth, slow and sleepy.

Dangling upside down,
it munches on red mangrove leaves.

Its fur is covered with green algae,
and it becomes one with the tree!

WHISPERS FROM THE TRIBE

A boat skims across the calm water.
The fisherman throws a net to catch shrimps.
Nearby, a woman scoops honey from the mangrove trees.

Little hands gently press a seed into the wet mud,
wanting many new mangrove trees to grow.
One day, these trees will spread their roots deep,
protecting them from storms and tide.

WHISPERS BY THE TREETOPS

A proboscis monkey leaps
to cross the river,
jiggling its big nose and round tummy
as it goes—SPLASH!

Giant saltwater crocodiles
lurk below, still as logs,
waiting to unleash their fiercest bite.

A monitor lizard rests in the tree trunk.
Its forked tongue flicks,
tasting the salty musk of crabs
skittering along the roots.

WHISPERS IN THE SHADOWS

As dusk falls, two cats—one big, one small—prowl the mangroves.

A tiger swishes its thick tail, making ripples across the water. There is no deer or boar to be found, so it's fish for now.

Nearby, a fishing cat crouches low.
With a swift swipe of its webbed paw,
it snatches a slippery catch!

WHISPERS OF THE NIGHT

In the deep night,
tiny sparks twinkle and glow.
Thousands of fireflies rise,
lighting up the dark mangroves.

Bats flutter through the trees,
hunting for their next meal.

WHISPERS OF NEW BEGINNINGS

In the morning, a tiny seedling drops from the tree. Plop! It floats on the waves across the oceans until it holds on to the land, spreading mangroves—

where every whisper
tells a story!

MANGROVES AROUND THE WORLD

Mangroves are superheroes! These amazing plants grow in warm, salty, muddy soil near water with extreme tides.

Spot mangrove forests on the map and see where they grow around the world. Many of them are at risk from the effects of climate change.

Mangroves help our planet – They absorb a lot of carbon, making our air clean and the earth cooler.

Mangroves stop the big waves – They block the storms and even tsunamis that try to crash onto the land.

Mangroves are water filters – Just like a sponge, mangroves soak up dirt and pollution, keeping our rivers, sea and ocean fresh.

Mangroves help people, too – They give us wood, medicine, and food like fish and honey.

Mangroves are home – Baby fishes, crabs, and baby sharks play and hide in their roots under the water. On land, they are home to many birds, snakes and even big animals.

ABOUT THE AUTHORS

Radhika Suri

With over three decades of experience, Radhika Suri is a passionate educator, author, and nature enthusiast. Her love for nature began on a rainy childhood day, watching tiny ants scurry about. That curiosity grew into a lifelong commitment, leading her to WWF India, where she spearheaded environmental education programs reaching millions of children across India. Today, she writes children's books that celebrate nature and India's rich culture, inspiring young minds to explore, dream, and create. Learn more at taleswithradhika.com.

Chetna Singh Kaith

With a background in Zoology and nearly a decade of experience, Chetna connects science, environment, and education to spark wonder in young minds. She finds joy in encouraging children to explore and protect the natural world. When she's not wandering through wild landscapes, she's sketching everything from tiny insects to majestic creatures, capturing nature's magic through her art.

ABOUT THE ILLUSTRATOR

Pari Satarkar

Pari Satarkar is a Pune-based animation filmmaker and illustrator with a deep love for the natural world. She runs Studio Mikudi, where she directs and produces original animated films, including her award-winning short 'Rising Tides', which explores marine ecology and coexistence. Her illustrations have appeared in children's books and projects with various wildlife organisations. When she's not drawing or animating, Pari can be found hanging out with her dog. See more of her work at @pari.jpeg on Instagram.